This booklet 'God is Love' is an op [...] a small community or individual [...] to grow in faith and to develop your [...] explored the scripture, with others or [...], [...] on the tradition and teaching of the Church, as summarised in the newly published *Compendium of the Catechism of the Catholic Church* or presented in Pope Benedict XVI's first encyclical *Deus Caritas Est* (DCE) from which this resource takes its name.

Towards the end of *Deus Caritas Est* the Holy Father reminds us that whatever we do in the way of good works will be lacking unless it is a true expression of love rooted in an encounter with Christ. That encounter with Christ is something Christ wishes for everyone, not just you and me, but for all the peoples of every nation. Why? Because there is no other name by which we shall be saved (Acts 4:12). All of us, as the Fathers of the Second Vatican Council remind us, stand in need of Christ, our model, our mentor, our liberator, our Saviour and the source of life (Decree *Ad Gentes* on the missionary activity of the church, 8).

'God is Love' is not intended to be a systematic study of *Deus Caritas Est,* rather, it is offered to you that in prayer and reflection you may grow in faith and understanding. Here may you encounter anew the Christ whose love has set us free. It is this same Christ we are called to share with our neighbour. Indeed, 'I cannot possess Christ just for myself; I can belong to him only in union with all those who have become, or who will become, his own' (DCE, 14).

With my blessing and prayers

Cardinal Cormac Murphy-O'Connor
Archbishop of Westminster

The meditation and faith sharing material found here has been co-authored by a group of people. In drawing this material together the group has been conscious of the desire expressed by many for 'more teaching'. Certainly, we would welcome your feedback at **evangelisation@rcdow.org.uk** or by post to the Agency for Evangelisation. A uniform structure has been observed throughout and we think you will be stimulated by the variety of styles and approaches to prayer.

- The **group session** begins with prayer, affording you the opportunity to give thanks, to ask forgiveness and to make your petitions to God. It is also a time to acknowledge before God, and those around you, the events of the past week, the present, as well as the needs of others. Following the scripture reading you are invited to share anything that has struck you. You are then offered a reflection that draws directly on *Deus Caritas Est*. Finally, having shared any further thoughts and questions, you are asked to tease out the implications which the scripture reading and reflection may have for Christian living in general and your life in particular. The group session concludes with a prayer which, for most weeks, is the same prayer the Holy Father uses to conclude *Deus Caritas Est*.

- The **daily meditation** begins with a short extract from the chosen Sunday Reading and is followed by a brief reflection. This reflection is complemented by an extract from *Deus Caritas Est* or the Compendium. Having spent some time reflecting on the scripture, you may want to spend some additional time reflecting on this particular text. A little later you may wish to look it up in the encyclical or the Compendium. Finally, there is a prayer to help you draw your daily meditation to a close.

The Church has always venerated the divine Scriptures just as she venerates the body of the Lord, since, especially in the sacred liturgy, she unceasingly receives and offers to the faithful the bread of life from the table both of God's word and of Christ's body. She has always maintained them, and continues to do so, together with sacred tradition, as the supreme rule of faith, since, as inspired by God and committed once and for all to writing, they impart the word of God Himself without change, and make the voice of the Holy Spirit resound in the words of the prophets and Apostles. Therefore, like the Christian religion itself, all the preaching of the Church must be nourished and regulated by Sacred Scripture. For in the sacred books, the Father who is in heaven meets His children with great love and speaks with them; and the force and power in the word of God is so great that it stands as the support and energy of the Church, the strength of faith for her sons, the food of the soul, the pure and everlasting source of spiritual life. Consequently these words are perfectly applicable to Sacred Scripture: 'For the word of God is living and active' (Hebrews 4:12) and 'it has power to build you up and give you your heritage among all those who are sanctified' (Acts 20:32; see Thessalonians 2:13).

Dei Verbum, 21.

Twenty-Ninth Sunday in Ordinary Time

Scripture from the 29th Sunday in Ordinary Time (Year B) - Mark 10:35-45

James and John, the sons of Zebedee, approached Jesus. 'Master,' they said to him 'we want you to do us a favour.' He said to them, 'What is it you want me to do for you?' They said to him, 'Allow us to sit one at your right hand and the other at your left in your glory.' 'You do not know what you are asking' Jesus said to them. 'Can you drink the cup that I must drink, or be baptised with the baptism with which I must be baptised?' They replied, 'We can.' Jesus said to them, 'The cup that I must drink you shall drink, and with the baptism with which I must be baptised you shall be baptised, but as for seats at my right hand or my left, these are not mine to grant; they belong to those to whom they have been allotted.'

When the other ten heard this they began to feel indignant with James and John, so Jesus called them to him and said to them, 'You know that among the pagans their so-called rulers lord it over them, and their great men make their authority felt. This is not to happen among you. No, anyone who wants to become great among you must be your servant, and anyone who wants to be first among you must be slave to all. For the Son of Man himself did not come to be served but to serve, and to give his life as a ransom for many.

Background

This episode took place whilst Jesus and his companions were on the road to Jerusalem. In the course of this journey Jesus spoke of the events which were to unfold in Jerusalem, but time and again his disciples failed to understand. Here Christ has to emphasise that a place in the kingdom will entail suffering. He also notes that he is not responsible for assigning status in the kingdom, and that service and humility rather than domination are to characterise the exercise of power and authority.

James and his brother John were Galilean fishermen and were among the first of the Apostles to be called by Jesus (Mark 1:19, Luke 5:1-11). Along with Peter they were particularly close to Christ. They were witnesses to Christ's transfiguration (Mark 9:2) and accompanied him in the garden of Gethsemane (Matt 26:37). John was to go with Peter to help prepare the upper room for the Passover meal or Last Supper (Luke 22:7-13). James and John seem to have been fairly fiery characters, asking Christ whether or not they should command fire to come down and consume a Samaritan village that refused to receive Christ (Luke 9:54). James would appear to have been the first of the apostles to be martyred, being killed by the sword (Acts 12:2).

From Deus Caritas Est

The one who serves does not consider himself superior to the one served…Christ took the lowest place in the world - the Cross - and by this radical humility he redeemed us and constantly comes to our aid. Those who are in a position to help others will realise that in doing so they themselves receive help; being able to help others is no merit or achievement of their own. This duty is a grace. The more we do for others, the more we understand and can appropriate the words of Christ: 'We are useless servants' (Luke 17:10). We recognise that we are not acting on the basis of any superiority or greater personal efficiency, but because the Lord has graciously enabled us to do so (DCE, 35).

Prayer

I offer you Lord,
my thoughts, to be fixed on you;
my words, to have you for their theme;
my actions, to be done according to your will;
my hardships, to be endured for your sake.

From the 'Universal Prayer' attributed to Pope Clement XI and found in the Divine Office under
'Thanksgiving after Mass'

James and John, the sons of Zebedee

Despite their lack of understanding and their getting things wrong, Jesus will still go on to entrust his mission to James and John. In doing so Christ issues us with both a challenge and a reassurance. The reassurance is that we do not have to be perfect to undertake the Lord's work. The challenge is that of delegating our work and responsibilities to others, even those who may have disappointed us in the past.

From Deus Caritas Est

In the end, we are only instruments in the Lord's hands; and this knowledge frees us from the presumption of thinking that we alone are personally responsible for building a better world. In all humility we will do what we can, and in all humility we will entrust the rest to the Lord. It is God who governs the world, not we (DCE, 35).

I offer you Lord,
my thoughts, to be fixed on you;
my words, to have you for their theme;
my actions, to be done according to your will;
my hardships, to be endured for your sake.

we want you to do us a favour

James' and John's request seems a little bold, even rude. They were not even asking for something essential or necessary. Yet, whatever the request, respectable or otherwise, what can any of us do before God, but beg a favour? God has given us life itself. What right have we to ask for anything more? Nonetheless, at the heart of the pattern of prayer given to us by Christ lies a straightforward invitation. 'Give us our daily bread' or more simply put, ask for what you need.

From the Compendium

553. What are the different forms of the prayer of petition? It can be a petition for pardon or also a humble and trusting petition for all our needs either spiritual or material. The first thing to ask for, however, is the coming of the Kingdom.

I offer you Lord,
my thoughts, to be fixed on you;
my words, to have you for their theme;
my actions, to be done according to your will;
my hardships, to be endured for your sake.

You do not know what you are asking

We ask because we do not know, because we are insecure. Inevitably there is the risk of rejection. Yet, even if they did not know what they were asking, the brothers' honesty is refreshingly frank and real. How often do we hide what we are really thinking or feeling? How often does the fear of ridicule keep us silent?

From the Compendium

521. What is one's duty towards the truth? Every person is called to sincerity and truthfulness in acting and speaking. Everyone has the duty to seek the truth, to adhere to it and to order one's whole life in accordance with its demands. In Jesus Christ the whole of God's truth has been made manifest. He is 'the truth'. Those who follow him live in the Spirit of truth and guard against duplicity, dissimulation, and hypocrisy.

I offer you Lord,
my thoughts, to be fixed on you;
my words, to have you for their theme;
my actions, to be done according to your will;
my hardships, to be endured for your sake.

Can you drink the cup that I must drink?

The cup which Jesus speaks of is the cup of suffering. It is never an easy cup to bear, but in calling on James and John to share in his suffering Jesus was not asking them to do anything that he himself would not do.

From the Compendium

123. Why does Jesus call upon his disciples to take up their cross? By calling his disciples to take up their cross and follow him Jesus desires to associate with his redeeming sacrifice those who are to be its first beneficiaries.

I offer you Lord,
my thoughts, to be fixed on you;
my words, to have you for their theme;
my actions, to be done according to your will;
my hardships, to be endured for your sake.

The cup that I must drink you shall drink

Instead of the seats they requested, Christ promised James and John a share in his suffering. James and John were not the only apostles to suffer. Moreover, down through the ages countless others have suffered in Christ's name. We too experience suffering and in the midst of that suffering Christ can seem a long way off. Here we are reminded of the fact that Christ embraced his suffering. He is not a passive bystander, cheering us on in the midst of our suffering; he is The Redeemer who has entered into the heart of our pain. When we, in suffering, are challenged to keep company with Him, remember he has already kept company with us.

From the Compendium

58. Why does God permit evil? Faith gives us the certainty that God would not permit evil if he did not cause a good to come from that very evil. This was realised in a wondrous way by God in the death and resurrection of Christ. In fact, from the greatest of all moral evils (the murder of his Son) he has brought forth the greatest of all goods (the glorification of Christ and our redemption).

I offer you Lord,
my thoughts, to be fixed on you;
my words, to have you for their theme;
my actions, to be done according to your will;
my hardships, to be endured for your sake.

to give his life as a ransom for many

Few, if any, of us will be asked to give up our lives for the Gospel, but the Gospel records how Jesus Christ did exactly this for all of us. The strength of his love cannot be doubted. Conscious of that love, how can I deny it to others? He died as a ransom for many and in keeping this good news to ourselves we deny to others the exhilarating truth of their being loved.

From Deus Caritas Est

Love promises infinity, eternity – a reality far greater and totally other than our everyday existence (DCE, 5).

I offer you Lord,
my thoughts, to be fixed on you;
my words, to have you for their theme;
my actions, to be done according to your will;
my hardships, to be endured for your sake.

Opening Prayer

Leader

Aloud or in the silence of our hearts let us bring to the Father our thanks (pause)…

Leader

In sorrow let us ask the Father for his forgiveness (pause)…

Leader

With confidence let us entrust to the Father our cares and concerns (pause)…

Leader

Heavenly Father, through the gift of your grace quieten our minds, open our hearts to your Word and our lives to your will, that we might flourish in our humanity and come to share in your divinity. We ask this through your Son, our Lord Jesus Christ, who lives and reigns with you and the Holy Spirit, one God, for ever and ever. Amen.

Explore the Scriptures from the 29th Sunday in Ordinary Time (Year B) - Mark 10: 35-45

James and John, the sons of Zebedee, approached Jesus. 'Master,' they said to him 'we want you to do us a favour.' He said to them, 'What is it you want me to do for you?' They said to him, 'Allow us to sit one at your right hand and the other at your left in your glory.' 'You do not know what you are asking' Jesus said to them. 'Can you drink the cup that I must drink, or be baptised with the baptism with which I must be baptised?' They replied, 'We can.' Jesus said to them, 'The cup that I must drink you shall drink, and with the baptism with which I must be baptised you shall be baptised, but as for seats at my right hand or my left, these are not mine to grant; they belong to those to whom they have been allotted.'

When the other ten heard this they began to feel indignant with James and John, so Jesus called them to him and said to them, 'You know that among the pagans their so-called rulers lord it over them, and their great men make their authority felt. This is not to happen among you. No; anyone who wants to become great among you must be your servant, and anyone who wants to be first among you must be slave to all. For the Son of Man himself did not come to be served but to serve, and to give his life as a ransom for many.

Following a short period of silence you may wish to share an image, a thought, a phrase or a question that has struck you.

From Deus Caritas Est

In *Deus Caritas Est* Pope Benedict reminds us that 'there will always be suffering which cries out for consolation and help. There will always be loneliness. There will always be situations of material need where help in the form of concrete love of neighbour is indispensable' (DCE, 28). He also reminds us that love or charity is that service which the Church renders in the face of want (DCE, 19). At the same time, though, the Holy Father is clear that our response to need and suffering is not simply a matter of doing something or making things better, of giving money or alleviating physical pain.

A Christian response to suffering must be rooted in prayer filled trust. It must also entail a sharing of our very selves, a self-giving in which we are personally present (DCE, 34). In calling on God, and giving of ourselves deeply and personally, the path we follow is the way of Christ. In the midst of his own suffering on the Cross he abandoned himself to the Father's will. He trusted and he called out. In healing the rift between us and God, in conquering our sin, our suffering and dying, he gave of himself.

Christ promised his disciples that they would suffer. When we proclaim God is love it is this which we are challenged to keep in view. To trust as Christ trusted. To give of ourselves as Christ gave of himself. Indeed, it was in this trusting and self-giving, where Christ takes on our pain and suffering, that the decisive turning point is reached. Suffering is transformed and the promise of a resurrected and eternal life is set before us.

In the Christian understanding suffering is far from pointless. It is full of opportunity. The opportunity to love. The opportunity to follow the way of Christ more fully. The opportunity of responding to another's need or, in the midst of our own suffering, of looking beyond ourselves just as Christ did. Indeed, from the Christian perspective, it is in this imitation of Christ's self-giving that the journey to self-discovery and to God opens up before us (DCE, 6).

Share your thoughts on this reflection from Deus Caritas Est. How does this week's scripture reading and reflection on Deus Caritas Est encourage you? How are you affirmed? In what ways are you challenged? What impact should this have on your daily living?

Closing Prayer

Holy Mary, Mother of God,
you have given the world its true light, Jesus, your Son – the Son of God.
You abandoned yourself completely to God's call
and thus became a wellspring of the goodness
which flows forth from him.
Show us Jesus. Lead us to him.
Teach us to know and love him,
so that we too can become capable of true love
and be fountains of living water in the midst of a thirsting world.

DCE, 42.

Thirtieth Sunday in Ordinary Time

Scripture from the 30th Sunday in Ordinary Time (Year B) - Mark 10: 46-52

As Jesus left Jericho with his disciples and a large crowd, Bartimaeus (that is, the son of Timaeus), a blind beggar, was sitting at the side of the road. When he heard that it was Jesus of Nazareth, he began to shout and say, 'Son of David, Jesus, have pity on me.' And many of them scolded him and told him to keep quiet, but he only shouted all the louder, 'Son of David, have pity on me.' Jesus stopped and said, 'Call him here.' So they called the blind man. 'Courage,' they said, 'get up; he is calling you.' So throwing off his cloak, he jumped up and went to Jesus. Then Jesus spoke, 'What do you want me to do for you?' 'Rabbuni,' the blind man said to him 'Master, let me see again.' Jesus said to him, 'Go; your faith has saved you.' And immediately his sight returned and he followed him along the road.

Background

In this passage Jesus continues his journey to Jerusalem. Jericho is fifteen miles north east of Jerusalem and five miles west of the River Jordan. In Mark's Gospel the healing of Bartimaeus can be contrasted with that of another blind man recounted in Mark 8: 22-26. We do not know the name of that blind man but we do know that his healing was a gradual process. The fact that Bartimaeus' healing was instantaneous rather than gradual may be explained by the relative strength of his faith. Certainly, Bartimaeus is the first to publicly address Jesus as the 'Son of David' and in so doing demonstrates a clear understanding of who Jesus was.

From the Compendium

314. What is the significance of Jesus' compassion for the sick? The compassion of Jesus towards the sick and his many healings of the infirm were a clear sign that with him had come the Kingdom of God and therefore victory over sin, over suffering, and over death. By his own passion and death he gave new meaning to our suffering which, when united with his own, can become a means of purification and of salvation for us and for others.

Prayer

Let me be your servant Lord,
let me rejoice not in myself
or in any other,
but in you,
because you alone are my real happiness;
you are my hope and my crown,
my joy and my honour.
Amen.

Adapted from Thomas À Kempis, The Imitation of Christ, Book III, Chapter 50.

Jesus left Jericho with his disciples and a large crowd

Bartimaeus' healing was a very public affair. It was not a private or romantic spectacle reserved for some tranquil spot. No, it was altogether more ordinary, taking place on the road before a large crowd. Certainly, Christ can be encountered in the peace and calm of a given place or certain time, but with Bartimaeus we must look for him where we are - in the heat and ordinariness of the day.

From Deus Caritas Est

Being Christian is not the result of an ethical choice or lofty idea, but the encounter with an event, a person, which gives life a new horizon and a decisive direction. Saint John's Gospel describes that event in these words: 'God so loved the world that he gave his only Son, that whoever believes in him should...have eternal life' (DCE, 1).

Heavenly Father,
guide me along the path of peace,
until I reach my true country,
the land of unending light.
Amen.

Adapted from Thomas À Kempis, The Imitation of Christ, Book III, Chapter 59.

he heard that it was Jesus of Nazareth

How did Bartimaeus come to hear that it was Jesus? Had people in the crowd been calling Christ's name or had someone taken the trouble to answer a question and tell him directly?

From the Compendium

80. How is the Good News spread? From the very beginning the first disciples burned with the desire to proclaim Jesus Christ in order to lead all to faith in him. Even today, from the loving knowledge of Christ there springs up in the believer the desire to evangelise and catechise, that is, to reveal in the Person of Christ the entire design of God and to put humanity in communion with him.

Sing a psalm to the Lord
for he has done glorious deeds,
make them known to all the earth!
People of Zion, sing and shout for joy
for great in your midst is the Holy One of Israel.

Isaiah 12:5-6

but he only shouted all the louder

Despite the protests of those in the crowd, Bartimaeus continued to shout all the louder. He was determined to be heard. The importance of being heard, listened to and acknowledged cannot be denied. But by the same token we must ask ourselves when and where we, like the crowd, have tried to silence a voice or more particularly, as in this instance, the voice that proclaims faith in Christ.

From the Compendium

365. Why does everyone have a right to exercise freedom? The right to the exercise of freedom belongs to everyone because it is inseparable from his or her dignity as a human person. Therefore this right must always be respected, especially in moral and religious matters, and it must be recognised and protected by civil authority within the limits of the common good and a just public order.

Lord hear my prayer,
let my cry for help reach you;
do not hide your face from me when I am in trouble;
bend down to listen to me,
when I call, be quick to answer me.

Psalm 102:1-2

Jesus stopped

It may be that this was an orderly crowd and that Bartimaeus' voice rang out loud and clear, but it is just as likely that his was one of many voices. Whether or not he was a lone voice Jesus stopped and gave Bartimaeus his undivided attention. Who was this Bartimaeus that Jesus should take the time to listen to him? The answer? A stranger to others, but not to Christ.

From Deus Caritas Est

There will always be suffering which cries out for consolation and help. There will always be loneliness. There will always be situations of material need where help in the form of concrete love of neighbour is indispensable. The State which would provide everything, absorbing everything into itself, would ultimately become a mere bureaucracy incapable of guaranteeing the very thing which the suffering person - every person - needs: namely, loving personal concern (DCE, 28).

Lord,
through the gift of your grace,
help me walk in the light of truth
- my heart enlightened, my burdens washed away -
that I may keep in mind
the good deeds to be done.
Amen.

Adapted from Thomas À Kempis, The Imitation of Christ, Book III, Chapter 55.

throwing off his cloak

It has been suggested that the cloak in question would have been the cloth that Bartimaeus used to collect the money given to him. As such, his throwing the cloak aside could be seen as an act of trust, a letting go of an old way of life to embrace something new...and all this before his sight had been restored!

From the Compendium

299. Do the baptised have need of conversion? The call of Christ to conversion continues to resound in the lives of the baptised. Conversion is a continuing obligation for the whole Church. She is holy but includes sinners in her midst.

O Most kind Jesus
be at my side,
share my labours
and be my constant companion.
May I will and desire
that which pleases you most.
Grant that in you,
and above all else,
I may find rest.
Amen.

Adapted from Thomas À Kempis, The Imitation of Christ, Book III, Chapter 15.

let me see again

In the course of this week's passage Bartimaeus shows himself to be a courageous and determined person. However in these few words 'let me see again' his courage, his determination, and his ability to trust is thrown into a whole new light. This is a truly remarkable man. At the very least, the trauma of losing his sight had not diminished his capacity to hope.

From the Compendium

387. What is hope? Hope is the theological virtue by which we desire and await from God eternal life as our happiness, placing our trust in Christ's promises and relying on the help of the grace of the Holy Spirit to merit it and to persevere to the end of our earthly life.

Gracious God,
grant me the grace
to serve you all the days of my life
and in serving you
to become truly free and truly holy.
Amen.

Adapted from Thomas À Kempis, The Imitation of Christ, Book III, Chapter 10.

Opening Prayer

Leader

Aloud or in the silence of our hearts let us bring to the Father our thanks (pause)...

Leader

In sorrow let us ask the Father for forgiveness (pause)...

Leader

With confidence let us entrust to the Father our cares and concerns (pause)...

Leader

Heavenly Father, through the gift of your grace quieten our minds, open our hearts to your Word and our lives to your will, that we might flourish in our humanity and come to share in your divinity. We ask this through your Son, our Lord Jesus Christ, who lives and reigns with you and the Holy Spirit, one God, for ever and ever. Amen.

Explore the Scripture from the 30th Sunday in Ordinary Time (Year B) Mark 10: 46-52

As Jesus left Jericho with his disciples and a large crowd, Bartimaeus (that is, the son of Timaeus), a blind beggar, was sitting at the side of the road. When he heard that it was Jesus of Nazareth, he began to shout and say, 'Son of David, Jesus, have pity on me.' And many of them scolded him and told him to keep quiet, but he only shouted all the louder, 'Son of David, have pity on me.' Jesus stopped and said, 'Call him here.' So they called the blind man. 'Courage,' they said, 'get up; he is calling you.' So throwing off his cloak, he jumped up and went to Jesus. Then Jesus spoke, 'What do you want me to do for you?' 'Rabbuni,' the blind man said to him 'Master, let me see again.' Jesus said to him, 'Go; your faith has saved you.' And immediately his sight returned and he followed him along the road.

Following a short period of silence you may wish to share an image, a thought, a phrase or a question that has struck you.

From Deus Caritas Est

In the Gospel passage we have read how Bartimaeus' faith had immediate consequences for his life. 'Go' says Christ, 'your faith has saved you'. In *Deus Caritas Est* Pope Benedict outlines the implications which our faith in Christ, our professed love of Christ, should have for us. Reminding us that we cannot possess Christ for ourselves he explains that being in Christ puts us in a relationship with everyone who claims Christ as a brother. Moreover, he defines the love of neighbour in even wider terms 'anyone who needs me, and whom I can help is my neighbour' (DCE, 15).

Loving our neighbour is not always a straightforward venture, particularly where we are at odds with them, but following the command to love is necessary if we are to grow in union with God. As the Holy Father explains, 'closing our eyes to our neighbour also blinds us to God' (DCE, 16). This union with God lies at the heart of our fulfilling the commandment to love and enables us to love those who we do not like or know. It is only on the basis of an intimate encounter with God, where 'our will and God's will increasingly coincide' to create 'a communion of will' that we can begin to look on others from the perspective of Jesus Christ, that Christ's friend can be seen as my friend (DCE, 17, 18). Indeed, it is only when we are in communion with God that we can truly engage with those we encounter. 'If I have no contact whatsoever with God in my life, then I cannot see in the other anything more than the other, and I am incapable of seeing in him the image of God' (DCE, 18).

Share your thoughts on this reflection from Deus Caritas Est. How does this week's scripture reading and reflection on Deus Caritas Est encourage you? How are you affirmed? In what ways are you challenged? What impact should this have on your daily living?

Closing Prayer

Holy Mary, Mother of God,
you have given the world its true light, Jesus, your Son – the Son of God.
You abandoned yourself completely to God's call
and thus became a wellspring of the goodness
which flows forth from him.
Show us Jesus. Lead us to him.
Teach us to know and love him,
so that we too can become capable of true love
and be fountains of living water in the midst of a thirsting world

DCE, 42.

Thirty First Sunday in Ordinary Time

Scripture from the 31st Sunday in Ordinary Time (Year B) – Mark 12:28-34

One of the scribes came up to Jesus and put a question to him, 'Which is the first of all the commandments?' Jesus replied, 'This is the first: *Listen, Israel, the Lord our God is the one Lord, and you must love the Lord your God with all your heart, with all your soul, with all your mind and with all your strength.* The second is this: *You must love your neighbour as yourself.* There is no commandment greater than these.' The scribe said to him, 'Well spoken, Master; what you have said is true: that he is one and there is no other. To love with all your heart and with all your understanding and strength and to love your neighbour as yourself, this is far more important than any holocaust or sacrifice.' Jesus, seeing how wisely he had spoken said, 'You are not far from the kingdom of God.' And after that no one dared to question him any more.

Background

During the course of his preaching, Jesus was frequently questioned by Old Testament Scripture scholars known as 'scribes'. In his Gospel, Mark recounted five of these encounters. They show how Jesus used the scriptures in his own teaching but they also show how opposition was growing among his opponents. These encounters were usually controversial, but in this particular episode the scribe agreed with Jesus who rooted his answer in the Old Testament (Deuteronomy 6:4-5; Leviticus 19:18). In his paraphrase of Jesus' statement, the scribe recognised that love of God and neighbour was of paramount importance.

From the Compendium

420. What is the New Law or the Law of the Gospels? The New Law or the Law of the Gospel, proclaimed and fulfilled by Christ, is the fullness and completion of the divine law, natural and revealed. It is summed up in the commandment to love God and neighbour and to love one another as Christ loved us. It is also an interior reality: the grace of the Holy Spirit which makes possible such love. It is 'the law of freedom' (Galatians 1:25) because it inclines us to act spontaneously by the prompting of charity.

Prayer

God our creator and sustainer,
breathe your Spirit upon us,
into our hearts, into our midst, into our work.
May your Spirit inspire all that we do
and the way that we do it.
May your Spirit work through each one of us,
to bring harmony among us and joy in our parish community.
Through Christ our Lord,
Amen.

From *Prayer for Parish Groups* by Donal Harrington and Julie Kavanagh, Columba Press, 1998

Listen, Israel

Jesus does not only invite the Chosen People - the Israelites - to listen to his message. Each one of us has been chosen and is being asked to still our hearts and minds in order to hear his teaching. In the words of Blessed Mother Teresa: 'We need silence to be alone with God, to speak to him, to listen to him, to ponder his words deep in our hearts.'

From the Compendium

571. What is contemplative prayer? Contemplative prayer is a simple gaze upon God in silence and love. It is a gift of God, a moment of pure faith during which the one praying seeks Christ, surrenders himself to the loving will of the Father, and places his being under the action of the Holy Spirit. Saint Teresa of Avila defines contemplative prayer as the intimate sharing of friendship, 'in which time is frequently taken to be alone with God who we know loves us.

Bless you Lord,
for this time of silence and for the space and peace it brings.
Help me to treasure the precious gift of silence
and to resist the temptation of putting it off until later.
As we discover you in the times of silence,
may our lives be blessed with new depth and tranquility.
Amen.

Adapted from *Prayer for Parish Groups* by Donal Harrington and Julie Kavanagh

all the commandments

Our faith is sometimes viewed as a list of legalistic obligations and prohibitions. Yet, because we have the gift of free choice, our daily living is our response to God's unconditional love. Everything we do is an act of turning to him or away from him.

From the Compendium

363. What is freedom? Freedom is the power given by God to act or not to act, to do this or to do that, and so to perform deliberate actions on one's own responsibility. Freedom characterises properly human acts. The more one does what is good, the freer one becomes. Freedom attains its proper perfection when it is directed towards God, the highest good and our beatitude. Freedom implies also the possibility of choosing between good and evil. The choice of evil is an abuse of freedom and leads to the slavery of sin.

Holy Spirit,
open our hearts and inspire our dreams.
Let fears be banished and hope ushered in.
According to your will,
grant us what courage and persistence we need
to make our dreams come true.
Holy Spirit,
inspire our imagination with new vision,
and breathe new passion into our lives.
Holy Spirit,
may the anticipation of the wonder of the kingdom
be the lifeblood of all our actions.
Amen.

Adapted from *Prayer for Parish Groups* by Donal Harrington and Julie Kavanagh

Jesus replied

As Christ replied to his questioner, we are called to respond to God's love. Through his earthly ministry, Jesus showed us how to live our lives in anticipation of and preparation for eternal life with him in heaven.

From the Compendium

232. What is the relationship between the sacraments and everlasting life? In the sacraments the Church already receives a foretaste of eternal life, while 'awaiting in blessed hope, the appearing in glory of our great God and saviour Christ Jesus' (Titus 2:13).

Lord our God,
help us to rest secure in your presence,
to acknowledge the signs of hope,
to live lives according to the Gospel
and to celebrate the Sacraments worthily.
Amen.

Adapted from *Prayer for Parish Groups* by Donal Harrington and Julie Kavanagh

the Lord our God is the one Lord

What are the golden calves and false gods pursued today? Where do lust, pride, anger, envy, avarice, sloth and gluttony figure in my life and society?

From the Compendium

443. What is the meaning of the words of our Lord, 'Adore the Lord your God and worship him alone' (Matthew 4:10)? These words mean to adore God as the Lord of everything that exists; to render to him the individual and community worship which is his due; to pray to him with sentiments of praise, of thanks, and of supplication; to offer him sacrifices, above all the spiritual sacrifice of one's own life, united with the perfect sacrifice of Christ; and to keep the promises and vows made to him.

O God,
I know that the path of life is full of hope and promise
if I travel with hope in you.
May I grow in trust that you will lead me
and do not allow me to be distracted by my own ambitions and desires.
May I follow wherever you may lead me.
Amen.

Adapted from *Prayer for Parish Groups* by Donal Harrington and Julie Kavanagh

You must love the Lord your God with all your heart

Proper food and rest support a strong, healthy heart to sustain our life here on earth. Acts of charity and prayer will nourish our heartfelt love for the Father as we journey towards life everlasting.

From the Compendium

9. What does the heart of Jesus exemplify? Jesus knew us and loved us with a human heart. His Heart, pierced for our salvation, is the symbol of that infinite love with which he loves the Father and each one of us.

We bless you Lord for our calling,
for nurturing in each of us a disciple's heart,
a heart that rejoices in your coming
a heart sustained by your Spirit
a heart encouraged by fellow disciples.
May there grow in each of our hearts
the disciple's commitment to serve,
the disciple's willingness to learn,
and the disciple's joy in becoming
a channel of your grace.

Adapted from *Prayer for Parish Groups* by Donal Harrington and Julie Kavanagh

with all your heart, with all your soul, with all your mind and with all your strength

We are to love God with our whole being. Nothing is hidden from God who can see into our hearts. He alone knows our innermost thoughts. There are times that our wants and desires are at odds with that of the Father.

From the Compendium

591. Why pray 'thy will be done on earth as it is in heaven'? The will of the Father is that 'all men be saved' (1 Timothy 2:4). For this Jesus came: to perfectly fulfill the saving will of his Father. We pray God our Father to unite our will to that of his Son after the example of the Blessed Virgin Mary and the saints. We ask that this loving plan be fully realised on earth as it is already in heaven. It is through prayer that we can discern 'what is the will of God' (Romans 12:2) and have the 'steadfastness' to do it (Hebrews 10:36).

Lifting our hearts and prayers to you, O God,
we remember that in days of old you gave a new heart to the people of Israel.
O God, give to us a renewed heart.
You gave a new heart to the disciples as they followed in the ways of Christ.
O God, give to us a renewed heart.
You gave a new heart to the martyrs as they stood firm and suffered for the love of the Gospel.
O God, give to us a renewed heart.
Ever faithful to the promises you made, you continue to give new heart to your people.
O God, give to us a renewed heart.
God of newness, renew our hearts, make us new.

Adapted from *Prayer for Parish Groups* by Donal Harrington and Julie Kavanagh

Opening Prayer

Leader

Aloud or in the silence of our hearts let us bring to the Father our thanks (pause)...

Leader

In sorrow let us ask the Father for forgiveness (pause)...

Leader

With confidence let us entrust to the Father our cares and concerns (pause)...

Leader

Heavenly Father, through the gift of your grace quieten our minds, open our hearts to your Word and our lives to your will, that we might flourish in our humanity and come to share in your divinity. We ask this through your Son, our Lord Jesus Christ, who lives and reigns with you and the Holy Spirit, one God, for ever and ever. Amen.

Explore the Scripture from the 31st Sunday in Ordinary Time (Year B) – Mark 12:28-34

One of the scribes came up to Jesus and put a question to him, 'Which is the first of all the commandments?' Jesus replied, 'This is the first: Listen, Israel, the Lord our God is the one Lord, and you must love the Lord your God with all your heart, with all your soul, with all your mind and with all your strength. The second is this: You must love your neighbour as yourself. There is no commandment greater than these.' The scribe said to him, 'Well spoken, Master; what you have said is true: that he is one and there is no other. To love with all your heart and with all your understanding and strength and to love your neighbour as yourself, this is far more important than any holocaust or sacrifice.' Jesus, seeing how wisely he had spoken said, 'You are not far from the kingdom of God.' And after that no one dared to question him any more.

Following a short period of silence you may wish to share an image, a thought, a phrase or a question that has struck you.

From Deus Caritas Est

'Listen, Israel, the Lord our God is the one Lord, and you must love the Lord your God with all your heart, with all your soul, with all your mind and with all your strength'. For us, the 'command' to love God may sound rather negative and unattractive. For the Jews however the Commandments were something to be loved and cherished. Given by God they are the way to life, a source of joy.

In *Deus Caritas Est*, Pope Benedict reminds us that loving as Christ loves – adhering to the Commandments - is the way to fulfilment and joy. We too have every reason to embrace the commandment to love. 'Love is indeed "ecstasy", not in the sense of a moment of intoxication, but rather as a journey, an ongoing exodus out of the closed inward-looking self towards its liberation through self-giving, and thus towards authentic self-discovery and indeed the discovery of God' (DCE, 6). That self-giving love should lead us to an understanding of ourselves should not be surprising. We are created in the image of God and everything we know of God is summed up in the Christ who gave of himself completely.

In setting this commandment before us, Christ is doing no more and no less than keeping our best interests at heart. Indeed, in commanding us to love, it is worth remembering the way in which God loves us. Ever generous he leaves us with the choice of picking up these commandments or putting them aside. In other words, love leaves the receiver free, or as Pope Benedict writes, 'it is not practised as a way of achieving other ends' (DCE, 31c).

Week Three Group Session

Share your thoughts on this reflection from Deus Caritas Est. How does this week's scripture reading and reflection on Deus Caritas Est encourage you? How are you affirmed? In what ways are you challenged? What impact should this have on your daily living?

Closing Prayer

Blessed be God eternal,
watching over all we do.
Blessed be Jesus,
our wisdom, companion in the striving.
Blessed be the divine Spirit,
constantly renewing our hearts.
Amen.

From *Prayer for Parish Groups* by Donal Harrington and Julie Kavanagh, Columbia Press, 1998

Thirty-Second Sunday in Ordinary Time

Scripture from the 32nd Sunday in Ordinary Time (Year B) - Hebrews 9: 24-28

It is not as though Christ had entered a man-made sanctuary which was only modelled on the real one: but it was heaven itself, so that he could appear in the actual presence of God on our behalf. And he does not have to offer himself again and again, like the high priest going into the sanctuary year after year with the blood that is not his own, or else he would have had to suffer over and over again since the world began. Instead of that, he has made his appearance once and for all, now at the end of the last age, to do away with sin by sacrificing himself. Since men only die once, and after that comes judgement, so Christ, too, offers himself only once to take the faults of many on himself, and when he appears a second time, it will not be to deal with sin but to reward with salvation those who are waiting for him.

Background

The first readers of this text were probably Christian Jews. The author did not write for all Jews. He wrote to a group, whom he knew well, that had become Christian. The book shows that they were not strong in their belief. They were in danger of going back to their old religion. The writer draws on images from the Old Testament which would have been familiar to Christians with Jewish roots. It would seem that he was writing before the fall of the Temple in Jerusalem which took place before AD 70.

At the time of writing these Christian Jews could not continue in Judaism and be Christians. They were faced with a choice; to go back to being Jews or to go on to be Christians. Indeed they could not keep on going to the temple as the Jews would not let them. The writer tries to show his readers that the right choice was to continue to trust in Jesus rather than hold on to the rituals and laws of their ancestors.

From the Compendium

169. What is the relationship of the Catholic Church with the Jewish people? The Catholic Church recognises a particular link with the Jewish people in the fact that God chose them before all others to receive his Word. To the Jewish people belong 'the sonship, the glory, the covenants, the giving of the law, the worship, the promises, and the patriarchs; and of their race according to the flesh, is the Christ' (Romans 9:4,5). The Jewish faith, unlike other non-Christian religions, is already a response to the Revelation of God in the Old Covenant.

Prayer

Grant Lord as we pray,
that as our faith is built on the Risen Christ,
so too may our hope be steadfast,
as we await the resurrection of your servants from the dead.
We make our prayer through Christ our Lord.
Amen.

From Morning Prayer for the Office for the Dead

It is not as though Christ has entered a man-made sanctuary

The sanctuaries in our churches, where the altar, lectern and priest's chair are situated, are man made. However, the sanctuary is not an ordinary place because it is here in the Mass, as the priest presides in the person of Christ, that we are given a foretaste of heaven.

From Deus Caritas Est

True no one has ever seen God as he is. And yet God is not totally invisible to us; he does not remain completely inaccessible (DCE, 17).

Father,
in your plan for salvation you have appointed priests
to minister to your people at your holy altars.
By the power of this sacrament
may their priestly service always be pleasing to you
and bring lasting good to your Church.
We ask this through Christ our Lord.
Amen.

The Prayer over the Gifts - Mass for Priests

And he does not have to offer himself again and again

In the Mass the sacrifice of Christ on the Cross is actually present to us. It is not merely a commemoration or a re-enactment of what happened on Good Friday. We believe that in the Mass we are present at the Last Supper, the passion and death of the Lord, and celebrating the resurrection. How then can the Mass be described as 'boring' if, like Mary his mother and John his beloved disciple, we stand at the foot of the Cross?

From the Compendium

276. Where does the Eucharist fit in the divine plan of salvation? The Eucharist was foreshadowed in the Old Covenant above all in the annual Passover meal celebrated every year by the Jews with unleavened bread to commemorate their hasty, liberating departure from Egypt. Jesus foretold it in his teaching and he instituted it when he celebrated the Last Supper with his apostles in a Passover meal. The Church, faithful to the command of her Lord, 'Do this in memory of me' (1 Corinthians:11:24), has always celebrated the Eucharist, especially on Sunday, the day of the Resurrection of Jesus.

Father
as your Son was raised on the cross,
his mother Mary stood by him, sharing his sufferings.
May your Church be united with Christ in his suffering and death,
and so come to share in his rising to new life
where he lives and reigns with you and the Holy Spirit,
one God, for ever and ever.
Amen.

Opening prayer - Feast of Our Lady of Sorrows

he has made his appearance once and for all

Jesus is the Word of God - God's final word - the perfect revelation of the Father's love. Private revelations to individuals, whether they are Saints or not, are offered to us to enrich this teaching and not to distract us from the chief sources of our knowledge of Christ.

From the Compendium

9. What is the full and definitive stage of God's Revelation? The full and definitive stage of God's revelation is accomplished in His Word made flesh, Jesus Christ, the mediator and fullness of Revelation. He, being the only-begotten Son of God made man, is the perfect and definitive Word of the Father. In the sending of the Son and the gift of the Spirit, Revelation is now fully complete, although the faith of the Church must grasp its full significance over the course of centuries. 'In giving us his Son, his only and definitive Word, God spoke everything to us at once in this sole Word, and he has no more to say' (St. John of the Cross) .

Almighty Father of our Lord Jesus Christ,
you have revealed the beauty of your power
by exalting the lowly virgin of Nazareth
and making her the mother of our saviour.
May the prayers of this woman bring Jesus to the waiting world
and fill the void of incompletion with the presence of her child,
who lives and reigns with you and the Holy Spirit,
one God, for ever and ever.
Amen.

Alternative Opening Prayer - Solemnity of the Annunciation

to do away with sin by sacrificing himself

St Ignatius of Antioch said of the Eucharist 'We break the one bread that provides the medicine of immortality, the antidote for death and the food that makes us live forever in Jesus Christ.'

From Deus Caritas Est

Jesus gave this act of oblation an enduring presence through his Institution of the Eucharist at the Last Supper. He anticipated his death and resurrection by giving his disciples, in the bread and wine, his very self, his body and blood as the new manna (DCE, 13).

Lord Jesus Christ,
you are the Holy Bread of life.
Bring to the glory of the resurrection
the people you have redeemed by the wood of the cross.
We ask this through Christ our Lord.
Amen.

Prayer over the Gifts - Triumph of the Cross

Since men only die once, and after that comes judgement

The most powerful weapon against evil is mercy. God is merciful and his complete desire is that each one of us be reconciled to him. Our own condemnation lies in our own refusal to embrace such loving mercy either now and at the hour of death.

From the Compendium

135. How will Christ judge the living and the dead? Christ will judge with the power he has gained as the Redeemer of the world who came to bring salvation to all. The secrets of hearts will be brought to light as well as the conduct of each one towards God and towards his neighbour. Everyone, according to how he has lived, will either be filled with life or damned for eternity. In this way the 'fullness of Christ' (Ephesians 4:13) will come about in which 'God will be all in all' (1 Corinthians 15:28).

Father of mercy,
in your great love for us
you have given us your only Son.
May he take us up into his own perfect sacrifice,
that we may offer you fitting worship.
We ask this through Christ our Lord.
Amen.

Prayer over the Gifts - Votive Mass of the Sacred Heart

and when he appears a second time, it will not be to deal with sin but to reward with salvation those who are waiting for him

Some scholars translate the final words of the above quotation as 'to save those who are eagerly waiting for him.' What does it mean to 'wait for the Lord'? Is my life a testimony to 'eagerly waiting' for the Lord's return?

From the Compendium

205. What happens to our body and soul after death? After death, which is the separation of the body and the soul, the body becomes corrupt while the soul, which is immortal, goes to meet the judgement of God and awaits its reunion with the body when it will rise transformed at the time of the return of the Lord. How the resurrection of the body will come about exceeds the possibilities of our imagination and understanding.

Father in heaven,
our hearts desire the warmth of your love
and our minds are searching for the light of your Word.
Increase our longing for Christ our Saviour
and give us the strength to grow in love,
that the dawn of his coming may find us rejoicing in his presence
and welcoming the light of his truth.
We ask this in the name of Jesus the Lord.
Amen.

Alternative Opening Prayer – First Sunday of Advent

Opening Prayer

Leader

In prayer let us bring to the Father our thanks...

Leader

In sorrow let us ask the Father for forgiveness....

Leader

With confidence let us entrust to the Father our cares and concerns.....

Leader

Heavenly Father, through the gift of your grace quieten our minds, open our hearts to your Word and our lives to your will, that we might flourish in our humanity and come to share in your divinity. We ask this through your Son, our Lord Jesus Christ, who lives and reigns with you and the Holy Spirit, one God, for ever and ever. Amen.

Explore the Scriptures from the 32nd Sunday in Ordinary Time (Year B) - Hebrews 9: 24-28

It is not as though Christ had entered a man-made sanctuary which was only modelled on the real one: but it was heaven itself, so that he could appear in the actual presence of God on our behalf. And he does not have to offer himself again and again, like the high priest going into the sanctuary year after year with the blood that is not his own, or else he would have had to suffer over and over again since the world began. Instead of that, he has made his appearance once and for all, now at the end of the last age, to do away with sin by sacrificing himself. Since men only die once, and after that comes judgement, so Christ, too, offers himself only once to take the faults of many on himself, and when he appears a second time, it will not be to deal with sin but to reward with salvation those who are waiting for him.

Following a short period of silence you may wish to share an image, a thought, a phrase or a question that has struck you.

From Deus Caritas Est

There is an old prayer to help the priest and servers prepare for Mass which goes: *'Go before us O Lord in this our sacrifice of prayer and praise, and grant that what we say and sing with our lips, we may believe in our hearts and that what we believe in our hearts, we may practice and show forth in our daily lives.'* In his teaching, Pope Benedict reminds us that our worship of God, even though it involves our time, energy and the giving of material goods, symbolised by the offering of bread and wine, will not reflect the truth of God's love unless our prayer and praise is accompanied by authentic self-giving love.

Every time we celebrate the Mass that self-giving love is set before us in the most graphic of ways; for here, the sacrifice of Christ on the Cross is made present. 'Jesus', as the Holy Father reminds us, 'gave this act of oblation (his self-offering) an enduring presence through his institution of the Eucharist at the Last Supper' (DCE, 13). In the Eucharist we stand at the foot of the Cross, we are faced with Love itself. A love in which there was no room for minimal or half-hearted gestures. Everything of Christ, for every one of us.

In *Deus Caritas Est,* Pope Benedict describes Christ's self-giving love as 'love in its most radical form' (DCE, 12). Yet, as we celebrate the Eucharist, we are much more than onlookers. Just as Christ brought himself whole and entire to the Cross, we are invited to bring ourselves whole and entire to the Eucharist. Here, as in Baptism, we are united with Christ. We enter into Christ's self-offering on the Cross, we feast on his body and blood, we share in his self-gift, there is 'union with God' (DCE, 13).

Because the Lord gives himself to us completely, nourishing and enriching us, we too must surely feel the same compulsion to give of ourselves physically in mind, heart and body to others. 'A Eucharist which does not pass over into the concrete practice of love is intrinsically fragmented' (DCE, 14). Yes, we can all say that we love God, but to learn to live in his love, to be in love with him, that requires a consistency of thought and action invoked in the traditional prayer of preparation, ... *'grant that what we say and sing with our lips, we may believe in our hearts and that what we believe in our hearts, we may practice and show forth in our daily lives'.*

Share your thoughts on this reflection from Deus Caritas Est. How does this week's scripture reading and reflection on Deus Caritas Est encourage you? How are you affirmed? In what ways are you challenged? What impact should this have on your daily living?

Closing Prayer

This is what I pray, kneeling before the Father, from whom every family, whether spiritual or natural takes its name: Out of his infinite glory, may he give you the power through his Spirit for your hidden self to grow strong, so that Christ may live in your hearts, through faith, and then, planted in love and built on love, you will with all the saints have strength to grasp the breadth and the length, the height and the depth; until knowing the love of Christ, which is beyond all knowledge, you are filled with the utter fullness of God. Amen

Ephesians 3: 14-19

Thirty-Third Sunday in Ordinary Time

Scripture from the 33rd Sunday in Ordinary Time (Year B) - Hebrews 10:11-14, 18

All the priests stand at their duties every day, offering over and over again the same sacrifices which are quite incapable of taking sins away. Christ, on the other hand, has offered one single sacrifice for sins, and then taken his place for ever, at the right hand of God, where he is now waiting until his enemies are made into a footstool for him. By virtue of that one single offering, he has achieved the eternal perfection of all whom he is sanctifying. When all sins have been forgiven, there can be no more sin offerings.

Background

The priests referred to in this passage were expected to offer up animal sacrifices --- goats and heifers - to God. Christ was a new kind of priest. He did not make a sacrifice of goats and heifers, he made a sacrifice of himself. In fact Christ was the perfect sacrifice - he is the Lamb without blemish – and because he was the perfect sacrifice, completely pleasing to God, no more animal sacrifices were needed after him. His blood has made us all holy and reconciled us to God.

From the Compendium

112: What is the importance of the Paschal Mystery of Jesus?
The Paschal Mystery of Jesus, which comprises his passion, death, Resurrection, and glorification, stands at the centre of the Christian faith because God's saving plan was accomplished once and for all by the redemptive death of his Son Jesus Christ.

Prayer

Lord Jesus Christ, fill me with your Holy Spirit. Let me listen with your ears and speak with your words in times of rest and activity. Bless all my encounters and conversations, and keep me in your embrace.

over and over again

At times it is difficult not to go over the past. It is difficult to let go of old wounds, but more especially to forgive ourselves for what we have got wrong and where we have let ourselves down. Yet, if we truly believe in the love and mercy of Christ's self-sacrifice on Calvary, we can place our trust in Christ, begin to let go, and move on. Do I feel guilty about past sins? Do I trust that Jesus can wipe the slate clean and that I can share in the glory that the Father has bestowed on his Son?

From the Compendium

391. What does the acceptance of God's mercy require from us? It requires that we admit our faults and repent of our sins. God himself by his Word and his Spirit lays bare our sins and gives us the truth of conscience and the hope of forgiveness.

Lord Jesus Christ,
fill me with your Holy Spirit.
Let me listen with your ears
and speak with your words
in times of rest and activity.
Bless all my encounters and conversations,
and keep me in your embrace.
Amen.

one single sacrifice

When we make sacrifices, when we give to others something of our time, our energy, our resources, joy enters into their lives. Moreover, their joy tends to be our joy. The single sacrifice spoken of here is the self-sacrifice of Christ, a sacrifice that gave way to the resurrection and the triumph over sin, death, and all that stands between us and God. In this 'one single sacrifice' everything is accomplished and our joy is complete because through Christ the way back to the Father is opened before us.

From Deus Caritas Est

Love of neighbour, grounded in the love of God, is first and foremost a responsibility for each individual member of the faithful (DCE, 20).

Lord Jesus Christ,
fill me with your Holy Spirit.
Let me listen with your ears
and speak with your words
in times of rest and activity.
Bless all my encounters and conversations,
and keep me in your embrace.
Amen.

taken his place for ever, at the right hand of God

Out of sight is out mind. It is a rare and precious friendship which survives the test of time and distance. Although he returned to the Father, Jesus did not abandon us. He continues at the right hand of God to intercede and to speak to his Father on our behalf. Who is it that I have left behind? Who is it that I would bring to the Father in prayer?

From Deus Caritas Est

It is time to reaffirm the importance of prayer in the face of the activism and the growing secularism of many Christians engaged in charitable work. Clearly, the Christian who prays does not claim to be able to change God's plans or correct what he has foreseen. Rather, he seeks an encounter with the Father of Jesus Christ, asking God to be present with the consolation of the Spirit to him and his work (DCE, 37).

Lord Jesus Christ,
fill me with your Holy Spirit.
Let me listen with your ears
and speak with your words
in times of rest and activity.
Bless all my encounters and conversations,
and keep me in your embrace.
Amen.

where he is now waiting

Christ waited for his disciples to understand. He waits for us to follow him and to grow in love of him. However Christ's waiting is not passive or disinterested. Through the Sacraments, Christ communicates the gift of his Spirit to us, he strengthens us, that we might be freed from that which hinders us in our journey to him. How conscious am I of the Holy Spirit at work in me? What have I achieved by God's grace?

From Deus Caritas Est

In the love-story recounted by the Bible, (God) comes towards us, he seeks to win our hearts, all the way to the Last Supper, to the piercing of his heart on the Cross, to his appearances after the Resurrection and to the great deeds by which, through the activity of the Apostles, he guided the nascent Church along its path... God does not demand of us a feeling which we ourselves are incapable of producing. He loves us, he makes us see and experience his love, and since he has 'loved us first', love can also blossom as a response within us (DCE, 17).

Lord Jesus Christ,
fill me with your Holy Spirit.
Let me listen with your ears
and speak with your words
in times of rest and activity.
Bless all my encounters and conversations,
and keep me in your embrace.
Amen.

he has achieved the eternal perfection

What better gift could there be than to be made perfect in the eyes of God? God may well love us as we are... and yet he loves us too much to let us stay as we are.

From the Compendium

2. Why does man have a desire for God? God himself, in creating man in his own image, has written upon his heart the desire to see him. Even if this desire is often ignored, God never ceases to draw man to himself because only in God will he find and live the fullness of truth and happiness for which he never stops searching. By nature and by vocation, therefore, man is a religious being, capable of entering into communion with God. This intimate and vital bond with God confers on man his fundamental dignity.

Lord Jesus Christ,
fill me with your Holy Spirit.
Let me listen with your ears
and speak with your words
in times of rest and activity.
Bless all my encounters and conversations,
and keep me in your embrace.
Amen.

When all sins have been forgiven, there can be no more sin offerings

Forgiven once and for all by God, what more is there to do but to give him thanks and praise?

From the Compendium

556. What is the prayer of praise? Praise is that form of prayer which recognises most immediately that God is God. It is a completely disinterested prayer: it sings God's praise for his own sake and gives him glory simply because he is.

Lord Jesus Christ,
fill me with your Holy Spirit.
Let me listen with your ears
and speak with your words
in times of rest and activity.
Bless all my encounters and conversations,
and keep me in your embrace.
Amen.

Opening Prayer

Leader

Aloud or in the silence of our hearts let us bring to the Father our thanks (pause)…

Leader

In sorrow let us ask the Father for forgiveness (pause)…

Leader

With confidence let us entrust to the Father our cares and concerns (pause)…

Leader

Heavenly Father, through the gift of your grace quieten our minds, open our hearts to your Word and our lives to your will, that we might flourish in our humanity and come to share in your divinity. We ask this through your Son, our Lord Jesus Christ, who lives and reigns with you and the Holy Spirit, one God, for ever and ever. Amen.

Explore the Scriptures from the 33rd Sunday in Ordinary Time (Year B) - Hebrews 10:11-14, 18

All the priests stand at their duties every day, offering over and over again the same sacrifices which are quite incapable of taking sins away. Christ, on the other hand, has offered one single sacrifice for sins, and then taken his place for ever, at the right hand of God, where he is now waiting until his enemies are made into a footstool for him. By virtue of that one single offering, he has achieved the eternal perfection of all whom he is sanctifying. When all sins have been forgiven, there can be no more sin offerings.

Week Five Group Session

Following a short period of silence you may wish to share an image, a thought, a phrase or a question that has struck you.

From Deus Caritas Est

Our giving can become a routine or formalistic affair - a habit we have got into, something we do over and over again, without thought, without love. In the foregoing reflections we have seen that for something to be a truly loving act it must be rooted in Christ (faith, prayer, the Eucharist), take us outside of ourselves (self-offering), be deeply personal (involving us on every level, emotional as well as physical), and leave the recipients completely free.

Even if we lived in a country or state where every material need was catered for and if we looked to the creation of 'just social structures' where works of charity were superfluous, there would still be a need for 'a service of love', for the Church 'alive with the love enkindled by the Spirit of Christ'. Man cannot live 'by bread alone' for we are more than things in need of material sustenance. 'The State which would provide everything, absorbing everything into itself, would ultimately become a mere bureaucracy incapable of guaranteeing the very thing which the suffering person - every person - needs; namely, loving personal concern' (DCE, 28b).

Share your thoughts on this reflection from Deus Caritas Est. How does this week's scripture reading and reflection on Deus Caritas Est encourage you? How are you affirmed? In what ways are you challenged? What impact should this have on your daily living?

Closing Prayer

Lord Jesus, help us to be aware of your love in every situation we face this week. Grant us the opportunity to bless others through our work, in our homes and parish communities and in every place we find ourselves. May your name be glorified and praised for ever. Amen.

Solemnity of our Lord Jesus Christ, Universal king

Scripture from the solemnity of Our Lord Jesus Christ, Universal King (Year B) - Apocalypse 1:5-8

Jesus Christ is the faithful witness, the First-born from the dead, the Ruler of the kings of the earth. He loves us and has washed away our sins with his blood, and made us a line of kings, priests to serve his God and Father; to him, then, be glory and power for ever and ever. Amen. It is he who is coming on the clouds; everyone will see him, even those who pierced him, and all the races of the earth will mourn over him. This is the truth. Amen. 'I am the Alpha and the Omega' says the Lord God, who is, who was, and who is to come, the Almighty.

Background

In exile on the island of Patmos John wrote the Book of the Apocalypse, also known as the Book of Revelation. Encouraging his fellow Christians in the midst of increasing persecution, he warned them of the dangers that could weaken their faith and dilute their love. The Apocalypse is the final book of the Bible and takes up the theme of creation spoken of in the first book of the Bible, the Book of Genesis. However, in the Apocalypse the creation referred to is the 'new' creation brought about through Christ's victory over sin and death on the Cross, which will reach its completion with the glorious second coming of our Lord Jesus Christ at the end of time.

From the Compendium

216. What is the hope of the new heavens and the new earth? After the final judgement the universe itself, freed from its bondage to decay, will share in the glory of Christ with the beginning of the 'new heavens' and a 'new earth' (2 Peter 3:13). Thus, the fullness of the Kingdom of God will come about, that is to say, the definitive realisation of the salvific plan of God to 'unite all things in Christ, things in heaven and things on earth' (Ephesians 1:10). God will then be 'all in all' (1 Corinthians 15:28) in eternal life.

Prayer

O my God,
I firmly believe that you are one God in three divine Persons,
Father, Son and Holy Spirit;
I believe that your divine Son became man and died for our sins,
and that he shall come to judge the living and the dead.
I believe these and all the truths that the Holy Catholic Church teaches,
because you have revealed them,
who can neither deceive nor be deceived.

Jesus Christ is the faithful witness

In his writings Cardinal Newman says 'God has created me to do some definite service he has not committed to another. I have my mission.' How am I being called to be a faithful witness to Christ in my words and actions today?

From the Compendium

190. How does the laity participate in the prophetic office? They participate in it by welcoming evermore in faith the Word of Christ and proclaiming it to the world by the witness of their lives, their words, their evangelising action, and by catechesis. This evangelising action always acquires a particular efficacy because it is accomplished in the ordinary circumstances of the world.

Direct, we beg you, O Lord,
our actions by your holy inspirations,
and grant that we may carry them out
with your gracious assistance,
that every prayer and work of ours
may begin always with you,
and through you be happily ended.
Amen.

the First-born from the dead

Tertullian, the early Church Father (c.155 – 230 AD) who introduced the word Trinity into the Christian vocabulary, said that 'The flesh is the hinge of salvation.' I am called in soul and body to share in the eternal life of heaven. I believe that everything about me, my soul and body, all that I am, will be raised on the last day, for I 'believe in the Word made flesh in order to redeem flesh' (*Compendium*, 202). In my thoughts, words and actions do I respect the body that will be raised on the last day?

From the Compendium

131. What is the saving meaning of the Resurrection? The Resurrection is the climax of the Incarnation. It confirms the divinity of Christ and all the things which he did and taught. It fulfils all the divine promises made for us. Furthermore the risen Christ, the conqueror of sin and death, is the principle of our justification and our resurrection. It procures for us now the grace of filial adoption which is a real share in the life of the only begotten Son. At the end of time he will raise up our bodies.

Lord God,
you prepared a worthy dwelling place for your Son
by the Immaculate Conception of the Virgin:
grant, we pray, that, as you preserved her from all stain of sin
in your foreknowledge of his death,
so we, by her intercession,
may come to you with pure hearts.
We ask this through Christ our Lord.
Amen.

He loves us and has washed away our sins with his blood

Fr Raniero Cantalamessa, preacher to the Papal Household, states that 'In the Mass it is possible for us to undergo each time a sort of spiritual dialysis: the debris of sin that accumulates in our conscience is dispelled by contact with the blood of Christ that comes into us under the sign of wine.' When tempted to sin I can call on the grace I have received through the Precious Blood in Holy Communion to purify my heart and my mind.

From the Compendium

85. Why did the Son of God become man? For us men and for our salvation, the Son of God became incarnate in the womb of the Virgin Mary by the power of the Holy Spirit. He did so to reconcile us sinners with God, to have us learn of God's infinite love, to be our model of holiness and to make us 'partakers of the divine nature' (2 Peter 1:4).

Lord, who hast form'd me out of mud,
and hast redeem'd me through thy blood,
and sanctifi'd me to do good:
purge all my sins done heretofore:
for I confess my heavy score,
and I will strive to sin no more.
Enrich my heart, mouth, hands in me,
with faith, with hope, with charity;
that I may run, rise, rest with thee.

George Herbert

and made us a line of kings

Through Baptism, we are called to share in the work of Christ and his threefold mission as priest, prophet and king. 'O Christian, be aware of your nobility – it is God's own nature that you share: do not then, by ignoble life, fall back into your former baseness. Think of the Head, think of the Body of which you are a member' (Pope St Leo the Great, 440-61).

From the Compendium

191. How do [the laity] participate in the kingly office? The laity participate in the kingly function of Christ because they have received from him the power to overcome sin in themselves and in the world by self-denial and the holiness of their lives. They exercise various ministries at the service of the community and they imbue temporal activities and the institutions of society with moral values.

Hail, Redeemer, King Divine!
Priest and Lamb, the throne is thine,
King, whose reign shall never cease,
Prince of everlasting peace.
Angels, saints and nations sing:
'Praised be Jesus Christ, our King;
Lord of life, earth, sky and sea,
King of love on Calvary.'

Patrick Brennan

priests to serve his God and Father

St Paul, in his letter to the Romans, urges his listeners to 'Present your bodies as a living sacrifice, holy and acceptable to God, which is your spiritual worship' (Romans 12:1). Each Friday, recalling the Passion of Christ, every adult Catholic is called to offer up some form of sacrifice, be it abstinence from some form of food, carrying out some penitential act, or undertaking some good and charitable work.

From the Compendium

189. How do the lay faithful participate in the priestly office of Christ? They participate in it especially in the Eucharist by offering as a spiritual sacrifice 'acceptable to God through Jesus Christ' (1 Peter 2:5) their own lives with all of their works, their prayers, their apostolic undertakings, their family life, their daily work and hardships borne with patience and even their consolations of spirit and body. In this way, even the laity, dedicated to Christ and consecrated by the Holy Spirit, offer to God the world itself.

O King of the Friday
whose limbs were stretched on the Cross,
O Lord who did suffer
the bruises, the wounds, the loss,
we stretch ourselves
beneath the shield of thy might,
some fruit from the tree of thy passion
fall on us this night!

Ancient Irish Prayer

to him, then, be glory and power for ever and ever. Amen.

Praised be Jesus Christ!

From the Compendium

217. What is the meaning of the word 'Amen' with which we conclude our profession of faith? The Hebrew word 'Amen', which also concludes the last book of Sacred Scripture, some of the prayers of the New Testament, and the liturgical prayers of the Church, expresses our confident and total 'yes' to what we professed in the Creed, entrusting ourselves completely to him who is the definitive 'Amen' (Revelation 3:14), Christ the Lord.

Holy is God! Holy and strong! Holy Immortal One,
have mercy on us.

To you, O Blessed Trinity,
be praise and honour and thanksgiving, for ever and ever!

Holy, holy, holy Lord, God of hosts.
Heaven and earth are filled with your glory.

Glory be to the Father and to the Son and to the Holy Spirit.
As it was in the beginning, is now, and ever shall be world without end.

Amen.

Opening Prayer

Leader

In prayer let us bring to the Father our thanks...

Leader

In sorrow let us ask the Father for forgiveness....

Leader

With confidence let us entrust to the Father our cares and concerns.....

Leader

Heavenly Father, through the gift of your grace quieten our minds, open our hearts to your Word and our lives to your will, that we might flourish in our humanity and come to share in your divinity. We ask this through your Son, our Lord Jesus Christ, who lives and reigns with you and the Holy Spirit, one God, for ever and ever. Amen.

Explore the Scripture from the solemnity of Our Lord Jesus Christ, Universal King (Year B) - Apocalypse 1:5-8

Jesus Christ is the faithful witness, the First-born from the dead, the Ruler of the kings of the earth. He loves us and has washed away our sins with his blood, and made us a line of kings, priests to serve his God and Father; to him, then, be glory and power for ever and ever. Amen. It is he who is coming on the clouds; everyone will see him, even those who pierced him, and all the races of the earth will mourn over him. This is the truth. Amen. 'I am the Alpha and the Omega' says the Lord God, who is, who was, and who is to come, the Almighty.

Following a short period of silence you may wish to share an image, a thought, a phrase or a question that has struck you.

From Deus Caritas Est

Christ is 'the faithful witness' and we, like the saints, are called to imitate Christ, to be bearers of light, men and women of faith, hope and love (DCE, 40). In *Deus Caritas Est* Pope Benedict reminds us that this light can be summed up in one word, LOVE. The invitation he issues is to experience that love – to accept the truth of our being loved – and so 'to cause the light of God to enter the world' (DCE, 39).

Prayer and the Eucharist are to be the bedrocks of all that we do. It is here that we will draw 'ever new strength' from Christ and that our capacity for loving will be renewed (DCE, 18, 36). Indeed, there is an 'unbreakable bond' between these two. 'Love of God and love of neighbour are…inseparable, they form a single commandment' (DCE 16,18).

Speaking at the beginning of Advent 1960 the future Pope Paul VI invited his listeners to refresh their faith and their love of God. In so doing he took up three themes that ring out again in Pope Benedict's encyclical.

a) to marvel 'I urge you above all to marvel, as if we were to come across something new.' The mysteries we celebrate throughout the Church's year are familiar yet 'the fountain is greater than my thirst' (St Augustine). These mysteries 'must become fresh again, immediate, and I must rejoice at their beauty, greatness, the miracle of the goodness of the Lord. To see! To see! To let our soul exult in the contact with the divine': 'the Lord God who is, who was, who is to come', (Apocalypse 1:8) who 'encounters us ever anew' (DCE, 17).

b) to strive to keep an ardent soul. To know. . . how to enjoy God. By this suggestion we may refresh our love of God. After our prayer or works of service 'let us also feel our love, love with the throbbing of our soul.' 'Thought must become emotion. . . to kindle the soul, like wood catching fire. So many times we put wood on and do not light it, for the spark is lacking. . . learn how to draw joy from our mysteries. What happiness awaits us!' because 'He loves us' (Apocalypse 1:5) and offers a love that 'comes from God and unites us to God' (DCE, 18).

c) to feel with certainty the new mission demanded of us. What might that mission be? It will be 'to serve his God and Father' (Apocalypse 1:6): 'To do all we can with what strength we have. . . is the task which keeps the good servant of Jesus Christ always at work: "The love of Christ urges us on" (2 Cor 5:14)' (DCE, 35).

Share your thoughts on this reflection from Deus Caritas Est. How does this week's scripture reading and reflection on Deus Caritas Est encourage you? How are you affirmed? In what ways are you challenged? What impact should this have on your daily living?

Closing Prayer

Holy Mary, Mother of God,
you have given the world its true light, Jesus, your Son – the Son of God.
You abandoned yourself completely to God's call
and thus became a wellspring of the goodness
which flows forth from him.
Show us Jesus. Lead us to him.
Teach us to know and love him,
so that we too can become capable of true love
and be fountains of living water in the midst of a thirsting world.

DCE, 42.

Notes

Notes

Notes

Notes

Notes

Notes

Notes

Notes

Notes